COME WITH ME

POEMS FOR A JOURNEY

By **Naomi Shihab Nye**
Images by **Dan Yaccarino**

Greenwillow Books
An Imprint of HarperCollinsPublishers

In memory of Kerry Stieler Crouch
Kerry picked up a chunky rectangular stone and
handed it over, saying, "Here, an elegant wristwatch . . .
next time I'll give you the band."
—N .S. N.

For Christopher Louis—
your journey has just begun
—D. Y..

The art was created as collages using mixed media.
The text type is Swiss 721 BT

Come with Me: Poems for a Journey
Text copyright © 2000 by Naomi Shihab Nye
Illustrations copyright © 2000 by Dan Yaccarino
Printed in Hong Kong by South China Printing Company (1988) Ltd.
All rights reserved.
www.harperchildrens.com

Library of Congress Cataloging-in-Publication Data
Nye, Naomi Shihab.
Come with me : poems for a journey / by Naomi Shihab Nye ;
images by Dan Yaccarino.
p.   cm.
"Greenwillow Books."
Summary: A collection of poems, including "Secrets,"
"When You Come to a Corner," "Mad," and "Come With Me."
ISBN 0-688-15946-X (trade).   ISBN 0-688-15947-8 (lib. bdg.)
1. Children's poetry, American.   [1. American poetry.]
I. Yaccarino, Dan, ill.   II. Title.
PS3564.Y44C66   2000   811'.54—dc21   99-34164   CIP

First Edition   10   9   8   7   6   5   4   3   2   1

CONTENTS

COME WITH ME

To the quiet minute between two noisy minutes
It's always waiting ready to welcome us
Tucked under the wing of the day
I'll be there
Where will you be?

OBSERVER

I watch how other things travel
to get an idea how I might move.
A cloud sweeps by silently,
gathering other clouds.
A doodlebug curls in his effort to get there.
A horse snorts before stepping forward.
A caterpillar inches across the kitchen floor.
When I carry him outside on a leaf,
I imagine someone doing that to me.
Would I scream?

In the heart of the day
nothing moves.
No one is going anywhere
or coming back.
The blue glass on the table
lets light pass through.
Something shines
but nothing moves.
I watch that too.

WHERE ARE WE GOING?

We are going up to the city that glitters,
carrying a pencil, a pillow, a blue tin cup.
And nothing that weighs us down.
And nothing that weighs us down.
A thousand people will pass us by
with their frowns and flickers and fancy shoes.
We'll walk and not walk
among the blinking, thinking signs.

Who will notice we've come to town?
Nobody, wonderful nobody.
Everything we thought we knew
is different here, and just as true.
We'll make notes on what we see.
Serving the hot dog with dignity.
Who is the person I'd find again?
Which eyes will I remember?

SPINNING

First you lie on your side
in the rumpled bed,
moving your thumb
and watching how you move it.
You stay that way for hours.

Later you crawl around on the floor.
There is a whole world under tables
and you find it.
Crumbs and threads and pennies.
You know what cats know.
People keep pulling you out.

Then you stand upright
like another kind of animal.
The days have steps in them,
slopes and curves.
You learn to do it all so quickly
you will barely remember not knowing.
You'll think you always climbed
the stairs two at a time.

Measuring in blocks how long it takes
to get somewhere, you never understand
        why it feels shorter coming home.

        First grade takes twenty years to get through.
                But second grade only takes ten.

                Gallop, slide, leap, stumble—
        so many words for the moves we make.
        Even when you stand in one place,
                things travel toward you—
                dust-motes in a light beam,
        rivers, the hands of the clock.

Was everything always moving to begin with?
                You know the earth was—secretly.
        And the air, and the rivers inside your body
                that you don't even feel.
                Are you a wheel spinning
                        in space?
Are you hooked to the slightest movement
        of a girl by the Arctic Sea?

SECRETS

One suitcase
only for secrets—
tucked in the pouch pocket,
pressed in the corners,
one light and liquid suitcase,
one glittering suitcase
filled with tiny
unspoken tales.

And I will carry it
to the other side of the ocean.
I will carry it
so no one knows
what I hold.
Because its cargo
is more precious than socks
or pajamas.
Because a secret is a ticket
and without it
the trip would be
too lonely.

He was old as a basket
and he carried more
than a basket carries.

Where he was going
tasted green and sweet
as the inside of a melon
that sleeps for days
in the sun.

His pants were gray flannel,
his sturdy heart a stem.
He remembered when the streets
were made of bricks.

For you he brought the fruit of papaya,
the yellow bell of the tree.
For you he brought a worn leash
to link you to your little dog.
No more little dogs for him.

He was old as a basket
and he carried the days
before you were born.

So you opened
your door
with a hundred
happy arms.

He sat in a chair
and made

a different

country

there.

WHEN YOU COME TO A CORNER

Do you turn?
Do you pause?
What if you can't bear
to leave the street you're on?
What if you love its old steps and porches and yards
and the name *Lucky Medina* scrawled in wet sidewalk cement in 1932,
and once you pressed your face to a certain tree trunk
when you were sad and it answered you?
(Whispering, "Yes.")

What if you have to move?

What if the houses around the corner
don't have any **Welcome** signs hanging out?
Their eyes are closed and you don't know the name
of anyone who lives here
and you never kicked your ball over their fence by mistake
and you're not sure where the curbs are
or the biggest dogs or the holes?

You still know your feet.

OUT THERE

The fallen tree
waits for us in the field.
Did lightning strike it
before we were born?
How could such a giant tree
lie down?

We climb and balance
on its craggy bark,
leaping from the high end
with our arms in the air,
yelling, "HO!"
Words taste better out there.

Where did all its leaves go?
All its branches and shade?
The tree became another tree.
We ride its huge back.
It makes us kings and queens.

Only my brother goes with me
wherever I go, like the other side
of the story.
We wear the light on our heads
till somebody calls us.
Everything we don't know
crawls into its hole.

SOMEBODY'S STORY

I started out singing
oh yes   oh yes
in a voice as clear
as a penny and a dime

in time   in time
I came to be
as tall as a riddle
as full as a shadow
as far as the wind
that blows itself
alone to the sea

I started out smiling
oh yes   oh yes
with my face tipped up
to the moon's soft stare
a halo of giggles
tied in my hair
with a sleep as deep
as desert sand

my dreams were the stories
that crossed the land

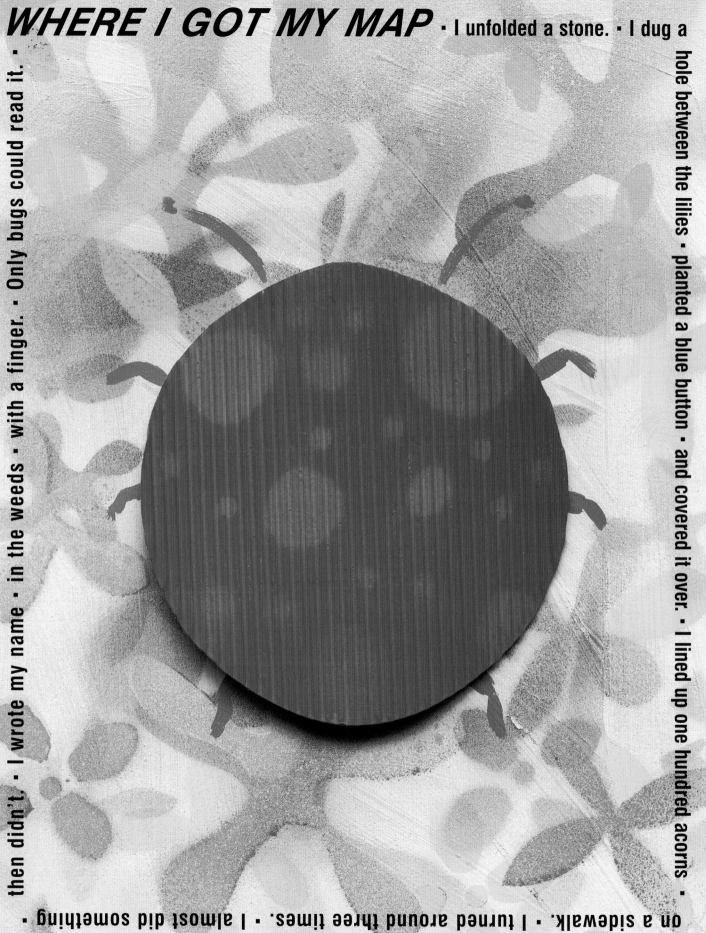

WHERE I GOT MY MAP

· I unfolded a stone. · I dug a hole between the lilies · planted a blue button · and covered it over. · I lined up one hundred acorns · on a sidewalk. · I turned around three times. · I almost did something · then didn't. · I wrote my name · in the weeds · with a finger. · Only bugs could read it. ·

COURAGE

A word must
travel through
a tongue and teeth
and wide air
to get there.
A word has
tough skin.

To be let in,
a word must slide
 and sneak
 and spin
  into the tunnel   of the   ear.

What's to fear?
Everything.
But a word
is brave.

SPRING RETURNS TO US
(AFTER HER LONG TRIP AROUND THE GLOBE)

Sun to skin:
> May I come in?
> Did you forget me?

Air to ear:
> Who's awake in here?
> Are you listening
> to the soft story
> we brought you
> as a souvenir?
> Listen—the day is deep.
> Can you swim?

Leaf to bough:
> I'm on my way!
> Forget the ice,
> I'll curl a little green today.

Bare feet to grass:
Remember me?
I feel like running far . . .
are you surprised?
I am—everything surprises me.

Bird-song to tree:
Can you translate?
I'm back, I trill, I eat,
and you look like home to me.

We followed
wisps of warm breeze.
Remember my tune?

Sun streams onto the bank.
The world is going on.
Everyone looks for something
small enough to thank.

FULL DAY

The pilot on the plane says:
In one minute and fifty seconds
we're going as far
as the covered wagon went
in a full day.

We look down
on clouds,
mountains of froth and foam.
We eat a neat
and subdivided lunch.

How was it for the people in
the covered wagon?
They bumped and jostled.
Their wheels broke.
Their biscuits were tough.
They got hot and cold and old.
Their shirts tore on the branches
they passed.

But they saw the pebbles
and the long grass
and the sweet shine of evening
settling on the fields.
They knew the ruts and the rocks.
They threw their furniture out
to make the wagons lighter.
They carried their treasures
in a crooked box.

ENVELOPE

The sky sends a letter to the ground.
Down, down from that high place
the giant page keeps shifting shapes,
moving around, thick waves of cloud
sent off to the edge of everywhere.

If you stare hard enough, you read
mountains, messages, feathers.
The story of roads
rolling in, drifting away.
Ripples and bits of song.

What did I do wrong?
Forget to say?
The sky erases it.

2.

Some days I try to clean my room
but there's confetti,
dirty socks, spoons, my little hedgehog,
peanut shells, pencils
under the bed.

Where did the brown crayons come from?
Whose shoes?

Mixed-up messy mush of stuff . . .
I get lost, looking.
Find my mother's silver scissors,
brother's twine.
Homework, birthday cards,
stones from an island,
stuffed bumblebee . . .
go outside for relief.
Stare up to read my mail.

No other letter
is better.

MAD

I got mad at my mother
so I flew to the moon.
I could still see our house
so little in the distance
with its pointed roof.
My mother stood in the front yard
like a pin dot
searching for me.
She looked left and right for me.
She looked deep and far.
Then I whistled and she tipped her head.
It gets cold at night on the moon.
My mother sent up a silver thread
for me to slide down on.
She knows me so well.
She knows I like silver.

31

TORN MAP

Once

by mistake

she tore a map

in half.

She taped it back,

but crookedly.

Now all the roads

ended in water.

There were mountains

right next to her hometown.

Wouldn't that be nice

if it were true?

I'd tear a map

and be right next

to you.

DATE DUE

12-13			
2/5/00			
5/20/02			
10-31-02			
521-03			
S-23			
1-21			
1/29/04			
1/30			
3-7-06			
12/13/10			

FOLLETT